Multiplication Facts: 2s and 3s

Practice the facts.

1. 2 x 1 = 2

2 x 2 = 4

2 x 3 = 6

2 x 4 = 8

2 x 5 = 10

2 x 6 = 12

2 x 7 = 14

2 x 8 = 16

2 x 9 = 18

Count by 2s to check your answers.

2. 3 x 1 = 3

3 x 2 = 6

3 x 3 = 9

3 x 4 = 12

3 x 5 = 15

3 x 6 = 18

3 x 7 = 21

3 x 8 = 24

3 x 9 = 27

Count by 3s to check your answers.

Toucan

4   6   8

If you change the order of the factors, the product is the same.

2 groups of 3   3 groups of 2

2 x 3 = 6   3 x 2 = 6

↑ ↑   ↑

factors product

This is the **commutative property** of multiplication.

3. 2 x 4 = 8   4 x 2 = 8

4. 3 x 6 = 18   6 x 3 = 18

5. 3 x 4 = 12   4 x 3 = 12

6. 7 x 2 = 14   2 x 7 = 14

7. 2 x 3 = 6   3 x 2 = 6

Multiplication facts: 2s and 3s; commutative property   3

Multiplication Facts: 4s and 5s

Practice the facts.

1. 4 x 1 = __4__
    4 x 2 = __8__
    4 x 3 = __12__
    4 x 4 = __16__
    4 x 5 = __20__
    4 x 6 = __24__
    4 x 7 = __28__
    4 x 8 = __32__
    4 x 9 = __36__

    Count by 4s to check your answers.

2. 5 x 1 = __5__
    5 x 2 = __10__
    5 x 3 = __15__
    5 x 4 = __20__
    5 x 5 = __25__
    5 x 6 = __30__
    5 x 7 = __35__
    5 x 8 = __40__
    5 x 9 = __45__

    Count by 5s to check your answers. The ones digit is _____ or _____ .

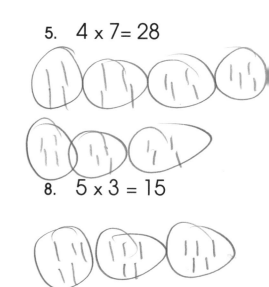

Ocelot

Draw groups of objects to show each multiplication fact.

3. 4 x 3 = 12

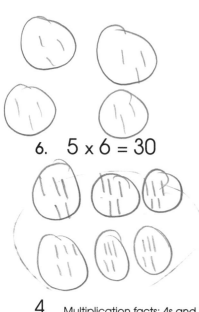

4. 5 x 4 = 20

5. 4 x 7 = 28

6. 5 x 6 = 30

7. 5 x 1 = 5

8. 5 x 3 = 15

Multiplication Facts: 0s and 1s

99%

5 groups of 0 objects is

$0 + 0 + 0 + 0 + 0 = 0.$

$5 \times 0 = 0$

And, $0 \times 0 = 0$

5 groups of 1 object is

$1 + 1 + 1 + 1 + 1 = 5.$

$5 \times 1 = 5$

And, $1 \times 5 = 5$

Practice the facts.

1. $0 \times 1 = 0$

    $0 \times 2 = 0$

    $0 \times 3 = 0$

    $0 \times 4 = 0$

    $0 \times 5 = 0$

    $0 \times 6 = 0$

    $0 \times 7 = 0$

    $0 \times 8 = 0$

    $0 \times 9 = 0$

2. $1 \times 1 = 1$

    $1 \times 2 = 2$

    $1 \times 3 = 3$

    $1 \times 4 = 4$

    $1 \times 5 = 5$

    $1 \times 6 = 6$

    $1 \times 7 = 7$

    $1 \times 8 = 8$

    $1 \times 9 = 9$

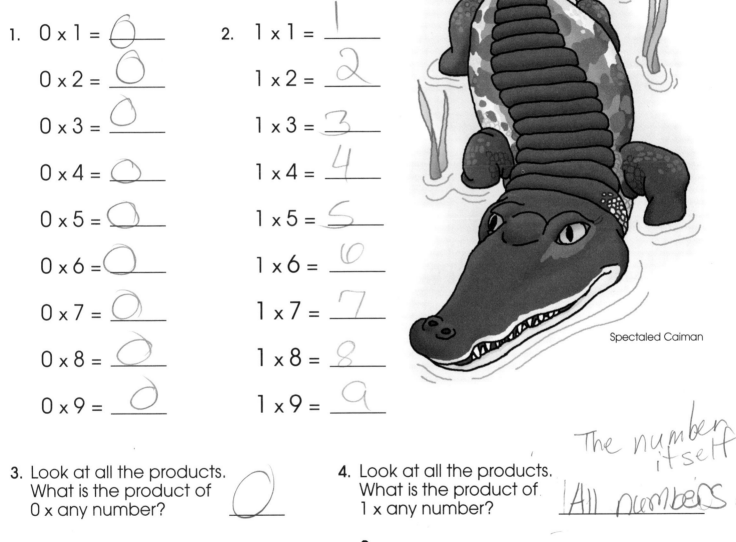

Spectaled Caiman

3. Look at all the products. What is the product of 0 x any number? 0

4. Look at all the products. What is the product of 1 x any number?

The number itself

All numbers.

Multiplication Facts: 6s and 7s

Practice the facts.

1. 6 x 0 = 0

   6 x 1 = 6

   6 x 2 = 12

   6 x 3 = 13

   6 x 4 = 24

   6 x 5 = 30

   6 x 6 = 36

   6 x 7 = 42

   6 x 8 = ___

   6 x 9 = ___

   Count by 6s to check your answers.

2. 7 x 0 = ___

   7 x 1 = ___

   7 x 2 = ___

   7 x 3 = ___

   7 x 4 = ___

   7 x 5 = ___

   7 x 6 = 42

   7 x 7 = ___

   7 x 8 = ___

   7 x 9 = ___

   Count by 7s to check your answers.

Pacu

Red Piranha

Jaraqui

---

3. Find as many multiplication facts as you can in this number search puzzle.

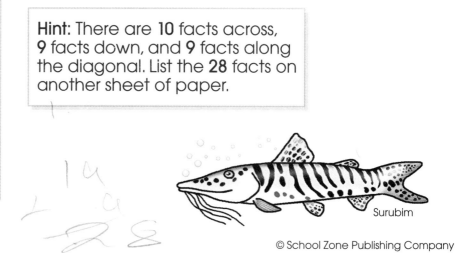

7	5	35	5	8	40	3	8
3	6	18	3	1	3	2	4
21	30	42	15	8	5	6	2
7	9	63	4	6	24	9	7
8	7	56	3	48	6	4	2
7	8	49	12	54	28	36	4
7	1	7	5	35	8	8	64

Hint: There are **10** facts across, **9** facts down, and **9** facts along the diagonal. List the **28** facts on another sheet of paper.

Surubim

Multiplication Facts: 8s and 9s

If you know your 4s facts, you can double them to know the 8s facts.

4 x 3 = 12
4 x 3 = 12
↓   ↓   ↓
8 x 3 = 24

Practice the facts.

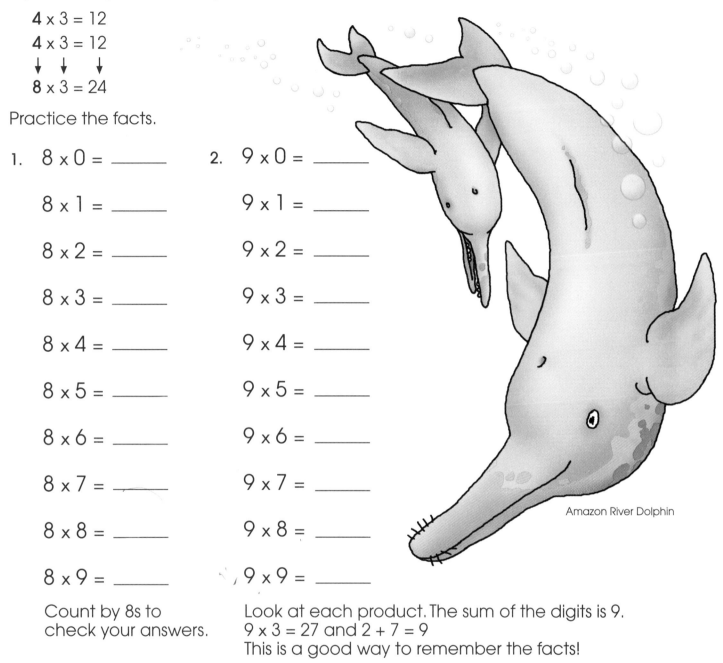

1. 8 x 0 = _____

    8 x 1 = _____

    8 x 2 = _____

    8 x 3 = _____

    8 x 4 = _____

    8 x 5 = _____

    8 x 6 = _____

    8 x 7 = _____

    8 x 8 = _____

    8 x 9 = _____

2. 9 x 0 = _____

    9 x 1 = _____

    9 x 2 = _____

    9 x 3 = _____

    9 x 4 = _____

    9 x 5 = _____

    9 x 6 = _____

    9 x 7 = _____

    9 x 8 = _____

    9 x 9 = _____

Amazon River Dolphin

Count by 8s to check your answers.

Look at each product. The sum of the digits is 9.
9 x 3 = 27 and 2 + 7 = 9
This is a good way to remember the facts!

Multiply.

3.

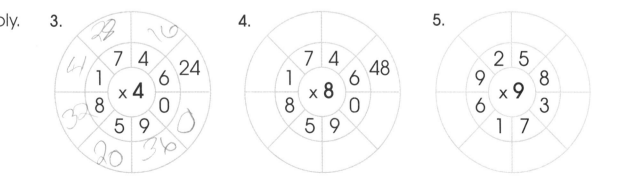

4.

5.

Multiplying with 10s

Find each amount in cents.

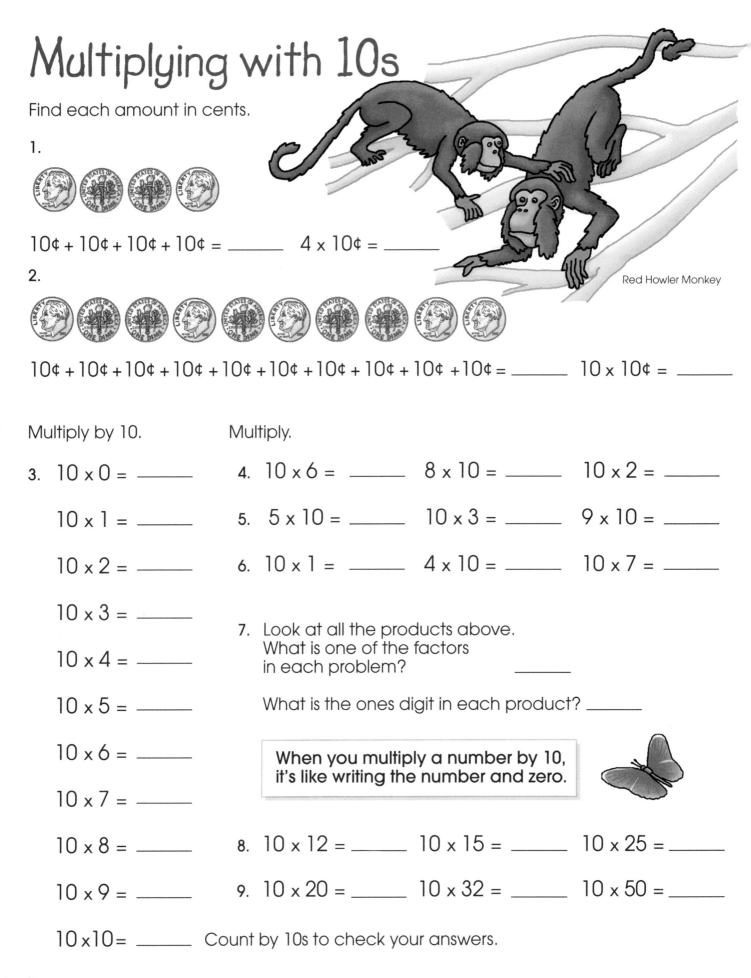

1.

$10¢ + 10¢ + 10¢ + 10¢ =$ _____ $4 \times 10¢ =$ _____

2.

$10¢ + 10¢ + 10¢ + 10¢ + 10¢ + 10¢ + 10¢ + 10¢ + 10¢ + 10¢ =$ _____ $10 \times 10¢ =$ _____

Red Howler Monkey

Multiply by 10.

3. $10 \times 0 =$ _____

$10 \times 1 =$ _____

$10 \times 2 =$ _____

$10 \times 3 =$ _____

$10 \times 4 =$ _____

$10 \times 5 =$ _____

$10 \times 6 =$ _____

$10 \times 7 =$ _____

$10 \times 8 =$ _____

$10 \times 9 =$ _____

$10 \times 10 =$ _____

Multiply.

4. $10 \times 6 =$ _____ $8 \times 10 =$ _____ $10 \times 2 =$ _____

5. $5 \times 10 =$ _____ $10 \times 3 =$ _____ $9 \times 10 =$ _____

6. $10 \times 1 =$ _____ $4 \times 10 =$ _____ $10 \times 7 =$ _____

7. Look at all the products above. What is one of the factors in each problem? _____

What is the ones digit in each product? _____

> When you multiply a number by 10, it's like writing the number and zero.

8. $10 \times 12 =$ _____ $10 \times 15 =$ _____ $10 \times 25 =$ _____

9. $10 \times 20 =$ _____ $10 \times 32 =$ _____ $10 \times 50 =$ _____

Count by 10s to check your answers.

Multiplying Up and Down

Multiplication problems can be written two ways.

$$\begin{array}{r} 4 \\ \times\ 3 \\ \hline 12 \end{array}$$ is the same as $3 \times 4 = 12$

Cyrbia

Scarce Bamboo

Cattie Heart

Tithorea

Brown Siproeta

Red Rim

Tiger Mimic

Orange Julia

Tailed Jay

Blue Morpho

Multiply.

1. $3 \times 2 =$ _____

2. $3 \times 9 =$ _____

3. $4 \times 5 =$ _____

4. $4 \times 9 =$ _____

5. $5 \times 6 =$ _____

6. $5 \times 9 =$ _____

7. $6 \times 2 =$ _____

8. $6 \times 7 =$ _____

9. $7 \times 4 =$ _____

10. $7 \times 8 =$ _____

11.
$$\begin{array}{r} 9 \\ \times\ 4 \\ \hline \end{array}$$

12.
$$\begin{array}{r} 8 \\ \times\ 5 \\ \hline \end{array}$$

13.
$$\begin{array}{r} 5 \\ \times\ 3 \\ \hline \end{array}$$

14.
$$\begin{array}{r} 8 \\ \times\ 4 \\ \hline \end{array}$$

15.
$$\begin{array}{r} 7 \\ \times\ 1 \\ \hline \end{array}$$

16.
$$\begin{array}{r} 8 \\ \times\ 7 \\ \hline \end{array}$$

17.
$$\begin{array}{r} 9 \\ \times\ 6 \\ \hline \end{array}$$

18.
$$\begin{array}{r} 5 \\ \times\ 0 \\ \hline \end{array}$$

19.
$$\begin{array}{r} 9 \\ \times\ 9 \\ \hline \end{array}$$

20.
$$\begin{array}{r} 9 \\ \times\ 8 \\ \hline \end{array}$$

21.
$$\begin{array}{r} 5 \\ \times\ 4 \\ \hline \end{array}$$

22.
$$\begin{array}{r} 6 \\ \times\ 6 \\ \hline \end{array}$$

Learning About Division

6 divided into 3 groups = 2 in each group

6 ÷ 3 = 2

6 divided by 2 in each group = 3 groups

6 ÷ 2 = 3

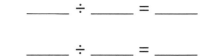

Complete each division problem.

1.

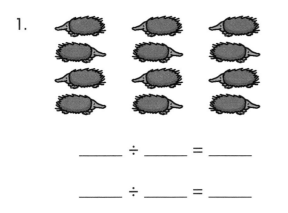

_____ ÷ _____ = _____

_____ ÷ _____ = _____

2.

_____ ÷ _____ = _____

_____ ÷ _____ = _____

3.

_____ ÷ _____ = _____

_____ ÷ _____ = _____

4.

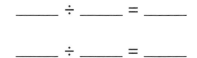

_____ ÷ _____ = _____

_____ ÷ _____ = _____

5.

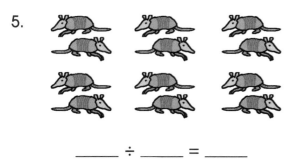

_____ ÷ _____ = _____

_____ ÷ _____ = _____

6.

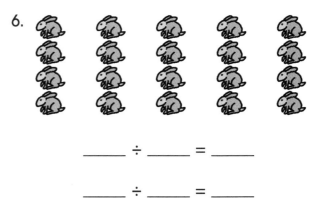

_____ ÷ _____ = _____

_____ ÷ _____ = _____

Learning About Division

If you know your multiplication facts, you are ready for division.

Here is a multiplication fact. **4 x 3 = 12**
Here are two related division facts. **12 ÷ 3 = 4** and **12 ÷ 4 = 3**

Hawk Headed Parrot

Write two related division facts for each multiplication fact.

1. 8 x 7 = 56

_____ ÷ _____ = _____

_____ ÷ _____ = _____

2. 4 x 9 = 36

_____ ÷ _____ = _____

_____ ÷ _____ = _____

3. 5 x 5 = 25

_____ ÷ _____ = _____

4. 6 x 7 = 42

_____ ÷ _____ = _____

_____ ÷ _____ = _____

5. 3 x 8 = 24

_____ ÷ _____ = _____

_____ ÷ _____ = _____

6. 2 x 7 = 14

_____ ÷ _____ = _____

_____ ÷ _____ = _____

7. 7 x 5 = 35

_____ ÷ _____ = _____

_____ ÷ _____ = _____

8. 8 x 9 = 72

_____ ÷ _____ = _____

_____ ÷ _____ = _____

9. 4 x 8 = 32

_____ ÷ _____ = _____

_____ ÷ _____ = _____

10. Joshua has collected **63** stamps from different countries.
    He has to divide them into **7** different albums. How many
    will go into each album?   _____

Multiplication and division are related   11

Dividing by 2s and 3s

There are **15** fish.

There are **3** groups.

$15 \div 3 = 5$

There are **5** fish in each group.

Clown Loach

Draw circles around groups of fish to show each division fact.
Then write the answer.

1. $14 \div 2 =$ _____

2. $12 \div 3 =$ _____

3. $8 \div 4 =$ _____

Practice these division facts. Recall related multiplication facts.

4. Divide

$2 \div 2 =$ _____

$4 \div 2 =$ _____

$6 \div 2 =$ _____

$8 \div 2 =$ _____

$10 \div 2 =$ _____

$12 \div 2 =$ _____

$14 \div 2 =$ _____

$16 \div 2 =$ _____

$18 \div 2 =$ _____

5. Divide

$3 \div 3 =$ _____

$6 \div 3 =$ _____

$9 \div 3 =$ _____

$12 \div 3 =$ _____

$15 \div 3 =$ _____

$18 \div 3 =$ _____

$21 \div 3 =$ _____

$24 \div 3 =$ _____

$27 \div 3 =$ _____

6. If you know $2 \times 8 = 16$,

then you know $16 \div 2 =$ _____

7. If you know $3 \times 7 = 21$, then

you know $21 \div$ _____ $=$ _____

8. If you know $2 \times 9 =$ _____ , then

you know _____ $\div 2 =$ _____

9. If you know _____ $\times 3 = 3$, then you

know _____ $\div$ _____ $=$ _____

Look at the facts above.

10. What is a number divided by itself? _____

Dividing by 4s and 5s

Circle the fish to show each division fact. Write the answer.

1. $20 \div 4 = \underline{\hspace{2cm}}$

2. $30 \div 5 = \underline{\hspace{2cm}}$

3. Divide.

$4 \div 4 = \underline{\hspace{1.5cm}}$

$8 \div 4 = \underline{\hspace{1.5cm}}$

$12 \div 4 = \underline{\hspace{1.5cm}}$

$16 \div 4 = \underline{\hspace{1.5cm}}$

$20 \div 4 = \underline{\hspace{1.5cm}}$

$24 \div 4 = \underline{\hspace{1.5cm}}$

$28 \div 4 = \underline{\hspace{1.5cm}}$

$32 \div 4 = \underline{\hspace{1.5cm}}$

$36 \div 4 = \underline{\hspace{1.5cm}}$

4. Divide.

$5 \div 5 = \underline{\hspace{1.5cm}}$

$10 \div 5 = \underline{\hspace{1.5cm}}$

$15 \div 5 = \underline{\hspace{1.5cm}}$

$20 \div 5 = \underline{\hspace{1.5cm}}$

$25 \div 5 = \underline{\hspace{1.5cm}}$

$30 \div 5 = \underline{\hspace{1.5cm}}$

$35 \div 5 = \underline{\hspace{1.5cm}}$

$40 \div 5 = \underline{\hspace{1.5cm}}$

$45 \div 5 = \underline{\hspace{1.5cm}}$

5. Practice the facts.

$12 \div 4 = \underline{\hspace{1.5cm}}$

$10 \div 5 = \underline{\hspace{1.5cm}}$

$32 \div 4 = \underline{\hspace{1.5cm}}$

$40 \div 5 = \underline{\hspace{1.5cm}}$

$4 \div 4 = \underline{\hspace{1.5cm}}$

$20 \div 5 = \underline{\hspace{1.5cm}}$

$36 \div 4 = \underline{\hspace{1.5cm}}$

$28 \div 4 = \underline{\hspace{1.5cm}}$

$5 \div 5 = \underline{\hspace{1.5cm}}$

$24 \div 4 = \underline{\hspace{1.5cm}}$

Surubim

Dividing by 6s and 7s

Giant Armadillo

Practice these division facts. Recall related multiplication facts.

1. Divide.

6 ÷ 6 = _____

12 ÷ 6 = _____

18 ÷ 6 = _____

24 ÷ 6 = _____

30 ÷ 6 = _____

36 ÷ 6 = _____

42 ÷ 6 = _____

48 ÷ 6 = _____

54 ÷ 6 = _____

2. Divide.

7 ÷ 7 = _____

14 ÷ 7 = _____

21 ÷ 7 = _____

28 ÷ 7 = _____

35 ÷ 7 = _____

42 ÷ 7 = _____

49 ÷ 7 = _____

56 ÷ 7 = _____

63 ÷ 7 = _____

3. Find the missing numbers.

36 ÷ _____ = 6

_____ ÷ 7 = 3

48 ÷ 6 = _____

_____ ÷ 7 = 7

18 ÷ _____ = 3

63 ÷ _____ = 9

21 ÷ _____ = 7

_____ ÷ 7 = 8

_____ ÷ 6 = 9

14   Dividing by 6s and 7s

Dividing by 8s and 9s

Banded Linsang

Practice these division facts. Recall related multiplication facts.

1. Divide.

8 ÷ 8 = _____

16 ÷ 8 = _____

24 ÷ 8 = _____

32 ÷ 8 = _____

40 ÷ 8 = _____

48 ÷ 8 = _____

56 ÷ 8 = _____

64 ÷ 8 = _____

72 ÷ 8 = _____

2. Divide.

9 ÷ 9 = _____

18 ÷ 9 = _____

27 ÷ 9 = _____

36 ÷ 9 = _____

45 ÷ 9 = _____

54 ÷ 9 = _____

63 ÷ 9 = _____

72 ÷ 9 = _____

81 ÷ 9 = _____

Fill in the missing numbers for each fact family.

3. 5 x 8 = _____   8 x _____ = 40

40 ÷ 5 = _____   40 ÷ 8 = _____

4. 9 x _____ = 54   6 x 9 = _____

54 ÷ 9 = _____   _____ ÷ 6 = 9

5. _____ x 8 = 72   8 x _____ = 72

72 ÷ 8 = _____   72 ÷ _____ = 8

6. 8 x 8 = _____   64 ÷ _____ = 8

Write a fact family for each group of numbers.

7. 7, 8, 56

_____ x _____ = _____

_____ x _____ = _____

_____ ÷ _____ = _____

_____ ÷ _____ = _____

8. 1, 9, 9

_____ x _____ = _____

_____ x _____ = _____

_____ ÷ _____ = _____

_____ ÷ _____ = _____

9. 0, 0, 8

_____ x _____ = _____

_____ x _____ = _____

_____ ÷ _____ = _____

Dividing with 1 and 0

$$5 \div 5 = 1 \qquad 5 \div 1 = 5$$

5 🐢 s divided into 5 groups

1 🐢 in each group

5 🐢 s divided into 1 group

5 🐢 s in the group

Yellow Spoted Turtle

1. Practice the facts. Match the fact to a division rule.

$4 \div 4 =$ _____

$0 \div 3 =$ _____

$7 \div 1 =$ _____

$2 \div 0 =$ _____

$8 \div 8 =$ _____

$0 \div 9 =$ _____

$6 \div 1 =$ _____

$0 \div 0 =$ _____

Here are some division rules.

Any number divided by
1 equals that number.
$5 \div 1 = 5$

Any non-zero number
divided by itself is 1.
$5 \div 5 = 1$

Zero divided by any non-zero
number equals 0.
$0 \div 5 = 0$

You cannot divide by zero.
You **cannot** do $5 \div 0$.

2. Try these! Match the problem to a division rule.

$10 \div 1 =$ _____

$12 \div 12 =$ _____

$0 \div 11 =$ _____

$25 \div 25 =$ _____

$15 \div 0 =$ _____

$0 \div 25 =$ _____

$12 \div 1 =$ _____

$11 \div 11 =$ _____

Writing Division Facts Two Ways

You can write a division problem two ways.
There are three parts to a division problem.

$12 \div 3 = 4$

Quotient
Divisor
Dividend

$3\overline{)12}$ ← Quotient
← Dividend

Divisor

Golden Lion Tamarin

Rewrite each division problem.

1. $36 \div 9 = 4$

2. $10 \div 2 = 5$

3. $56 \div 8 = 7$

4. $63 \div 7 = 9$

Complete the problems by finding a **divisor** and a **quotient**.

5. $18 \div \underline{\hspace{1cm}} = \underline{\hspace{1cm}}$

6. $\underline{\hspace{1cm}}\overline{)30}$

7. $\underline{\hspace{1cm}}\overline{)45}$

8. $54 \div \underline{\hspace{1cm}} = \underline{\hspace{1cm}}$

9. $72 \div \underline{\hspace{1cm}} = \underline{\hspace{1cm}}$

10. $\underline{\hspace{1cm}}\overline{)7}$

Find each quotient.

11. $36 \div 4 = \underline{\hspace{1cm}}$

12. $6\overline{)42}$

13. $27 \div 3 = \underline{\hspace{1cm}}$

14. $7\overline{)63}$

15. $56 \div 8 = \underline{\hspace{1cm}}$

16. $9\overline{)81}$

17. $8\overline{)8}$

18. $40 \div 5 = \underline{\hspace{1cm}}$

19. $6\overline{)0}$

Multiplication & Division Facts Puzzle

Complete each problem.
Then write the numbers in the puzzle.

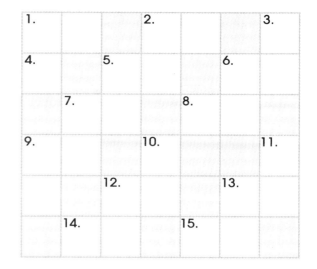

Across

1. 5 groups of 8 is _____ .

2. 7 x 8 = _____

3. 27 ÷ 9 = _____

4. 8 x _____ = 64

5. _____ ÷ 6 = 4

6. 9 groups of 4 is _____ .

7. 2 x 7 = _____

8. 5 x 4 = _____

9. 9 x 8 = _____

10. 6 ÷ _____ = 6

11. _____ x 5 = 30

12. 4 x 7 = _____

13. _____ ÷ 4 = 6

14. 8 x 5 = _____

15. _____ ÷ 7 = 4

Jaguarmundi

Down

1. 8 x 6 = _____

2. _____ ÷ 6 = 9

3. 6 x 6 = _____

5. _____ ÷ 8 = 3

6. 5 groups of 6 is _____ .

7. _____ ÷ 3 = 4

9. _____ ÷ 8 = 9

10. 3 groups of 6 is _____ .

11. _____ ÷ 8 = 8

12. 5 x 4 = _____

13. 4 x 7 = _____

Multiplication and division facts review

Multiplying 2-Digit Numbers

If you know the multiplication facts, you can multiply any two numbers together.

Multiply the **ones**.

Tens Ones

$$
\begin{array}{r}
2\;3 \\
\times\quad 3 \\
\hline
9
\end{array}
$$

Multiply the **tens**.

Tens Ones

$$
\begin{array}{r}
2\;3 \\
\times\quad 3 \\
\hline
6\;9
\end{array}
$$

Quetzal

Multiply.

1.
$$
\begin{array}{r} 14 \\ \times\;\;2 \\ \hline \end{array}
\qquad
\begin{array}{r} 12 \\ \times\;\;4 \\ \hline \end{array}
\qquad
\begin{array}{r} 23 \\ \times\;\;2 \\ \hline \end{array}
$$

2.
$$
\begin{array}{r} 33 \\ \times\;\;3 \\ \hline \end{array}
\qquad
\begin{array}{r} 24 \\ \times\;\;2 \\ \hline \end{array}
\qquad
\begin{array}{r} 11 \\ \times\;\;7 \\ \hline \end{array}
$$

3.
$$
\begin{array}{r} 32 \\ \times\;\;3 \\ \hline \end{array}
\qquad
\begin{array}{r} 10 \\ \times\;\;4 \\ \hline \end{array}
\qquad
\begin{array}{r} 13 \\ \times\;\;2 \\ \hline \end{array}
$$

4. Up to **3** plant and animal species are becoming extinct each day. How many could be extinct in **12** days?

_____

Multiplying with Regrouping

Sometimes you need to regroup when you multiply.

Multiply the **ones**.
Regroup.

$$\begin{array}{r} {\scriptstyle 3} \\ 4\,5 \\ \times\ \ 7 \\ \hline 5 \end{array}$$

Multiply the **tens**.
Add regrouped ones.

$$\begin{array}{r} {\scriptstyle 3} \\ 4\,5 \\ \times\ \ 7 \\ \hline 3\,1\,5 \end{array}$$

7 x 5 = 35 ones
Regroup as 3 tens
and 5 ones.

7 x 4 = 28 tens
28 + 3 = 31 tens
31 tens is 3 hundreds
and 1 ten.

Paca

Multiply.

1.
$$\begin{array}{r} 42 \\ \times\ \ 6 \\ \hline \end{array}$$
$$\begin{array}{r} 98 \\ \times\ \ 2 \\ \hline \end{array}$$
$$\begin{array}{r} 74 \\ \times\ \ 4 \\ \hline \end{array}$$
$$\begin{array}{r} 34 \\ \times\ \ 3 \\ \hline \end{array}$$
$$\begin{array}{r} 78 \\ \times\ \ 2 \\ \hline \end{array}$$
$$\begin{array}{r} 64 \\ \times\ \ 5 \\ \hline \end{array}$$

2.
$$\begin{array}{r} 63 \\ \times\ \ 9 \\ \hline \end{array}$$
$$\begin{array}{r} 18 \\ \times\ \ 3 \\ \hline \end{array}$$
$$\begin{array}{r} 55 \\ \times\ \ 5 \\ \hline \end{array}$$
$$\begin{array}{r} 19 \\ \times\ \ 9 \\ \hline \end{array}$$
$$\begin{array}{r} 28 \\ \times\ \ 3 \\ \hline \end{array}$$
$$\begin{array}{r} 45 \\ \times\ \ 5 \\ \hline \end{array}$$

Try these!

3. 4 x 2 x 3 = _____   5 x 2 x 8 = _____   6 x 2 x 3 = _____

Multiplying 3-Digit Numbers

Estimate the product: 6 x 452 is about 6 x 500 = 3,000.

Multiply the ones.
Regroup.

$$\begin{array}{r} \overset{1}{4}5\overset{}{2} \\ \times\quad 6 \\ \hline 2 \end{array}$$

6 x 2 = 12 ones
Regroup as 1 ten
and 2 ones.

Multiply the tens.
Add regrouped ones.
Regroup.

$$\begin{array}{r} \overset{3}{4}\overset{1}{5}2 \\ \times\quad 6 \\ \hline 12 \end{array}$$

6 x 5 = 30 tens
30 + 1 = 31 tens
Regroup as 3
hundreds and 1 ten.

Multiply the hundreds.
Add regrouped tens.

$$\begin{array}{r} \overset{3}{4}\overset{1}{5}2 \\ \times\quad 6 \\ \hline 2,712 \end{array}$$

6 x 4 = 24 hundreds
24 + 3 = 27 hundreds

Estimate the product. Then multiply.

1. Estimate

    $$\begin{array}{r} 126 \\ \times\quad\quad \end{array} \qquad \begin{array}{r} 126 \\ \times\quad 4 \\ \hline \end{array}$$

    Estimate

    $$\begin{array}{r} 472 \\ \times\quad\quad \end{array} \qquad \begin{array}{r} 472 \\ \times\quad 2 \\ \hline \end{array}$$

    Estimate

    $$\begin{array}{r} 975 \\ \times\quad\quad \end{array} \qquad \begin{array}{r} 975 \\ \times\quad 4 \\ \hline \end{array}$$

2. Estimate

    $$\begin{array}{r} 134 \\ \times\quad\quad \end{array} \qquad \begin{array}{r} 134 \\ \times\quad 7 \\ \hline \end{array}$$

    Estimate

    $$\begin{array}{r} 813 \\ \times\quad\quad \end{array} \qquad \begin{array}{r} 813 \\ \times\quad 3 \\ \hline \end{array}$$

    Estimate

    $$\begin{array}{r} 144 \\ \times\quad\quad \end{array} \qquad \begin{array}{r} 144 \\ \times\quad 8 \\ \hline \end{array}$$

3. Estimate

    $$\begin{array}{r} 135 \\ \times\quad\quad \end{array} \qquad \begin{array}{r} 135 \\ \times\quad 2 \\ \hline \end{array}$$

    Estimate

    $$\begin{array}{r} 292 \\ \times\quad\quad \end{array} \qquad \begin{array}{r} 292 \\ \times\quad 5 \\ \hline \end{array}$$

    Estimate

    $$\begin{array}{r} 224 \\ \times\quad\quad \end{array} \qquad \begin{array}{r} 224 \\ \times\quad 9 \\ \hline \end{array}$$

Multiplying 4-Digit Numbers

$$\begin{array}{r} {\scriptstyle 2\ \ 1\ 1} \\ 5{,}432 \\ \times\qquad 6 \\ \hline 32{,}592 \end{array}$$

Multiply the **ones**. Regroup.
Multiply the **tens**. Regroup.
Multiply the **hundreds**. Regroup.
Multiply the **thousands**. $6 \times 5 = 30 + 2 = 32$.

Multiply.

1.

$$\begin{array}{r} 2{,}222 \\ \times\quad 3 \\ \hline \end{array}\qquad \begin{array}{r} 3{,}141 \\ \times\quad 5 \\ \hline \end{array}\qquad \begin{array}{r} 1{,}338 \\ \times\quad 6 \\ \hline \end{array}$$

2.

$$\begin{array}{r} 9{,}214 \\ \times\quad 4 \\ \hline \end{array}\qquad \begin{array}{r} 7{,}768 \\ \times\quad 2 \\ \hline \end{array}\qquad \begin{array}{r} 5{,}261 \\ \times\quad 3 \\ \hline \end{array}$$

3.

$$\begin{array}{r} 3{,}105 \\ \times\quad 7 \\ \hline \end{array}\qquad \begin{array}{r} 2{,}025 \\ \times\quad 8 \\ \hline \end{array}\qquad \begin{array}{r} 6{,}350 \\ \times\quad 5 \\ \hline \end{array}$$

4. The largest reptile is the saltwater crocodile.
   It weighs **1,150** pounds. How much would a half
   dozen of them weigh?

_____

Saltwater Crocodile

Multiplying by 2-Digit Numbers

Multiply by ones to find a partial product.

$$\begin{array}{r} {}^{3} \\ 54 \\ \times\ 38 \\ \hline 432 \end{array}$$

$8 \times 54 = 432$

Multiply by tens to find another partial product.

$$\begin{array}{r} {}^{1} \\ 54 \\ \times\ 38 \\ \hline 432 \\ 1620 \end{array}$$

3 tens x 54 = 162 tens
162 tens is 1620

Add the partial products.

$$\begin{array}{r} 54 \\ \times\ 38 \\ \hline 432 \\ +\ 1620 \\ \hline 2,052 \end{array}$$

Victoria Crowned Pigeon

Multiply. Estimate the products to check your answers.

1.

$$\begin{array}{r} 31 \\ \times\ 77 \\ \hline \end{array}$$
Estimate
x _____

$$\begin{array}{r} 46 \\ \times\ 22 \\ \hline \end{array}$$
Estimate
x _____

$$\begin{array}{r} 93 \\ \times\ 11 \\ \hline \end{array}$$
Estimate
x _____

2.

$$\begin{array}{r} 84 \\ \times\ 17 \\ \hline \end{array}$$
Estimate
x _____

$$\begin{array}{r} 53 \\ \times\ 44 \\ \hline \end{array}$$
Estimate
x _____

$$\begin{array}{r} 62 \\ \times\ 25 \\ \hline \end{array}$$
Estimate
x _____

3. Joshua has **23** classmates. He promised to send each of them a postcard from all of the **12** cities he plans to visit. How many postcards will he send? _____

Dividing by 1-Digit Numbers

When you divide, there are five steps to remember.
Repeat them over and over until you finish dividing.

Humming Bird

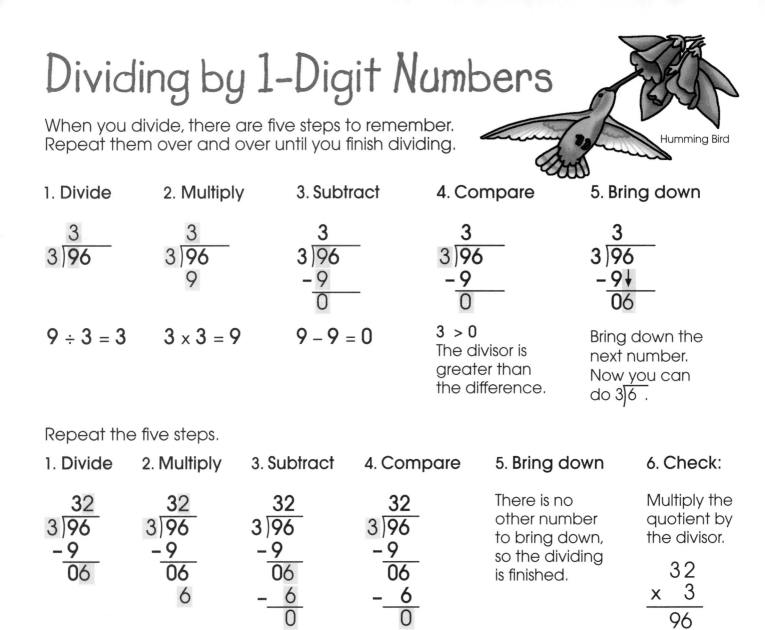

1. Divide	2. Multiply	3. Subtract	4. Compare	5. Bring down
$\begin{array}{r} 3 \\ 3\overline{)96} \end{array}$	$\begin{array}{r} 3 \\ 3\overline{)96} \\ 9 \end{array}$	$\begin{array}{r} 3 \\ 3\overline{)96} \\ -9 \\ \hline 0 \end{array}$	$\begin{array}{r} 3 \\ 3\overline{)96} \\ -9 \\ \hline 0 \end{array}$	$\begin{array}{r} 3 \\ 3\overline{)96} \\ -9\downarrow \\ \hline 06 \end{array}$
$9 \div 3 = 3$	$3 \times 3 = 9$	$9 - 9 = 0$	3 > 0 The divisor is greater than the difference.	Bring down the next number. Now you can do $3\overline{)6}$.

Repeat the five steps.

1. Divide	2. Multiply	3. Subtract	4. Compare	5. Bring down	6. Check:
$\begin{array}{r} 32 \\ 3\overline{)96} \\ -9 \\ \hline 06 \end{array}$	$\begin{array}{r} 32 \\ 3\overline{)96} \\ -9 \\ \hline 06 \\ 6 \end{array}$	$\begin{array}{r} 32 \\ 3\overline{)96} \\ -9 \\ \hline 06 \\ -6 \\ \hline 0 \end{array}$	$\begin{array}{r} 32 \\ 3\overline{)96} \\ -9 \\ \hline 06 \\ -6 \\ \hline 0 \end{array}$	There is no other number to bring down, so the dividing is finished.	Multiply the quotient by the divisor. $\begin{array}{r} 32 \\ \times\ 3 \\ \hline 96 \end{array}$

Divide. Then check your answer.

1. $2\overline{)84}$ Check

   $\times$ _____

2. $4\overline{)92}$ Check

   $\times$ _____

3. $8\overline{)96}$ Check

   $\times$ _____

4. $3\overline{)57}$ Check

   $\times$ _____

5. $5\overline{)95}$ Check

   $\times$ _____

6. $7\overline{)84}$ Check

   $\times$ _____

Quotients with Remainders

Tailed Jay

Sometimes a division problem has a **remainder**.

If **23** frogs were divided into groups of **3**, there would be **7** groups of **3**, and **2** frogs **remaining**.

The **R** stands for **Remainder**.

```
    7 R 2
3)23
  -21
    2
```

Check: Multiply the quotient by the divisor. Then add the remainder.

```
    7
  x 3
   21
  + 2
   23
```

Divide. Then check your answer.

1. 4)47   Check:

2. 6)56   Check:

3. 5)29   Check:

4. 2)95   Check:

5. 7)89   Check:

6. 6)82   Check:

7. 4)39   Check:

8. 3)67   Check:

9. 5)52   Check:

Dividing 3-Digit Numbers

Look closely at these two problems.
This one has a quotient with 3 digits.

This one has a quotient with 2 digits.

```
   124 R3        Check:
5)623
 -5             124
 ---          x   5
 12            -----
-10             620
 ---          +   3
 23            -----
-20             623
 ---
   3
```

> Remember to do the five steps of division over and over.

Coati

```
    84 R3        Check:
5)423
-40              84
 ---           x  5
 23            -----
-20             420
 ---          +   3
   3           -----
                423
```

Divide. Then check your answer.

1. 4)936   Check:

2. 4)336   Check:

3. 4)446   Check:

4. 6)249   Check:

5. 7)665   Check:

6. 3)940   Check:

7. 8)890   Check:

8. 9)621   Check:

9. 7)688   Check:

Zeros in the Quotient

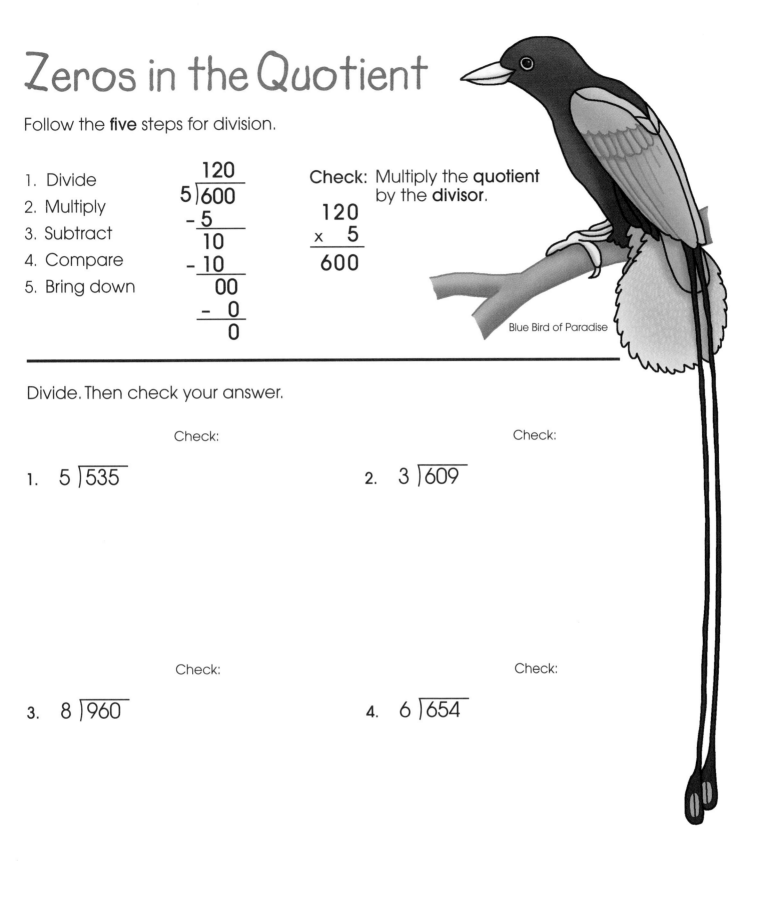

Follow the **five** steps for division.

1. Divide
2. Multiply
3. Subtract
4. Compare
5. Bring down

```
      120
  5 )600
    - 5
      10
    - 10
      00
     - 0
       0
```

Check: Multiply the **quotient** by the **divisor**.

```
   120
 x   5
   600
```

Blue Bird of Paradise

Divide. Then check your answer.

Check:

1. 5)535

Check:

2. 3)609

Check:

3. 8)960

Check:

4. 6)654

5. Joshua's family traveled **720** miles in **3** days. How many miles did they average each day? _____

Division Review

Divide. Match the letters of the quotients to the numbers below.

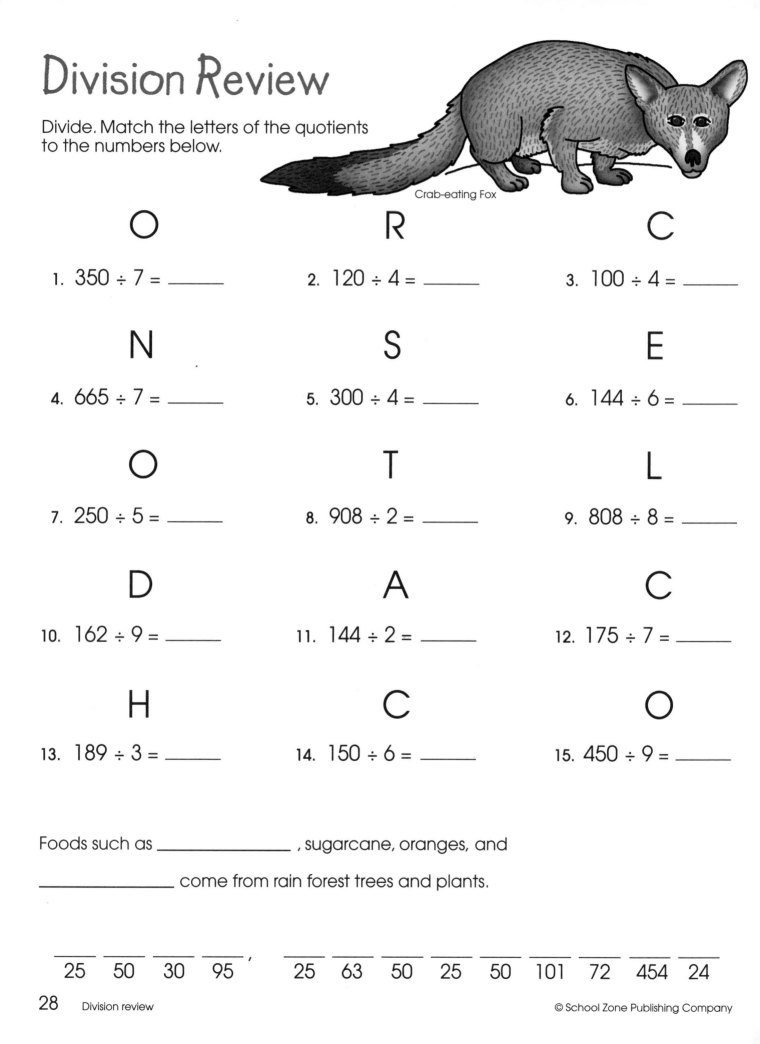

Crab-eating Fox

O
1. 350 ÷ 7 = _____

R
2. 120 ÷ 4 = _____

C
3. 100 ÷ 4 = _____

N
4. 665 ÷ 7 = _____

S
5. 300 ÷ 4 = _____

E
6. 144 ÷ 6 = _____

O
7. 250 ÷ 5 = _____

T
8. 908 ÷ 2 = _____

L
9. 808 ÷ 8 = _____

D
10. 162 ÷ 9 = _____

A
11. 144 ÷ 2 = _____

C
12. 175 ÷ 7 = _____

H
13. 189 ÷ 3 = _____

C
14. 150 ÷ 6 = _____

O
15. 450 ÷ 9 = _____

Foods such as _____ , sugarcane, oranges, and

_____ come from rain forest trees and plants.

___ ___ ___ ___ , ___ ___ ___ ___ ___ ___ ___ ___ ___
25 50 30 95   25 63 50 25 50 101 72 454 24

What I Learned About Division

Estimate the quotient.

1. $38 \div 6$ is about _____ .

2. $8\overline{)66}$ is about _____ .

Spot-billed Toucanet

Divide. Then check your answer.

Check:

3. $4\overline{)95}$

Check:

4. $6\overline{)723}$

Check:

5. $8\overline{)302}$

Check:

6. $6\overline{)642}$

Check:

7. $4\overline{)688}$

Check:

8. $3\overline{)811}$

Divide. Show your work.

9. $7\overline{)91}$

10. $4\overline{)862}$

11. $6\overline{)58}$

12. $5\overline{)107}$

13. $6\overline{)820}$

14. $5\overline{)940}$

15. $8\overline{)275}$

16. $4\overline{)312}$

17. $9\overline{)803}$

18. $6\overline{)555}$

19. $7\overline{)808}$

20. $3\overline{)625}$

Multiplication and Division Puzzle

Work the problems out on another piece of paper
to find the answers to the puzzle.

Across

1. 346 x 8

5. 4⟌148

7. 2 x 407

8. 900 ÷ 6

9. 6 x 0

10. 75 x 40

12. 9 x 407

13. 6⟌3,126

16. 800 x 3

18. 9 x 81

19. 107 x 8

Down

1. 9⟌252

2. 355 x 2

3. 8 x 8

4. 50 x ___ = 400

5. 7,006 x 5

6. 700 ÷ 1

8. 848 ÷ 8

10. 4 x 9

11. 3 x 509

14. 4⟌968

15. 654 ÷ 6

17. 8⟌368

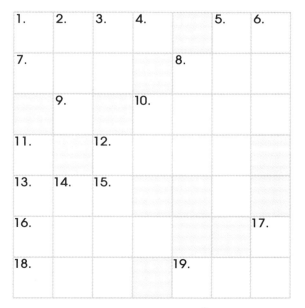

1.	2.	3.	4.		5.	6.
7.				8.		
	9.		10.			
11.		12.				
13.	14.	15.				
16.						17.
18.			19.			

Mandrill